THE CHICAGO BEARS

Sloan MacRae

PowerKiDS press™

New York

Published in 2011 by The Rosen Publishing Group, Inc.
29 East 21st Street, New York, NY 10010

First Edition

Editor: Amelie von Zumbusch
Book Design: Greg Tucker
Layout Design: Julio Gil

Photo Credits: Cover (Sid Luckman), p. 22 (top) Vic Stein/Getty Images; cover (Jay Cutler, background), pp. 7, 21 Scott Boehm/Getty Images; cover (Walter Payton), p. 17 Ronald C. Modra/Sports Imagery/ Getty Images; p. 5 Joe Robbins/Getty Images; p. 9 Dilip Vishwanat/Getty Images; p. 11 Chicago History Museum/Getty Images; p. 13 Getty Images/Getty Images; p. 15 Vernon Biever/Getty Images; p. 19 Jonathan Daniel/Getty Images; p. 22 (bottom) Getty Images Sport/Getty Images.

Library of Congress Cataloging-in-Publication Data

MacRae, Sloan.
  The Chicago Bears / by Sloan MacRae. — 1st ed.
      p. cm. — (America's greatest teams)
  Includes index.
  ISBN 978-1-4488-2580-6 (library binding) — ISBN 978-1-4488-2749-7 (pbk.) —
ISBN 978-1-4488-2750-3 (6-pack)
  1. Chicago Bears (Football team)—Juvenile literature. I. Title. II. Series.
  GV956.C5M33 2011
  796.332'640977311—dc22

2010035360

Manufactured in the United States of America
CPSIA Compliance Information: Batch #113160PK: For Further Information contact Rosen Publishing, New York, New York at 1-800-237-9932

CONTENTS

CHANGING THE GAME

The Chicago Bears are one of the most important teams in the history of **professional** football. Some of the greatest players and **coaches** of all time have been Chicago Bears. The Bears are one of the oldest teams in the National Football League, or the NFL. The Bears helped the young game of American football grow into the sport we know today. They changed the way that football is played forever.

The Bears have one of the richest histories in American sports. They are also one of the NFL's most successful teams. Over the years, they have won more games than any other team in the NFL!

Players for the Bears have set many records. Devin Hester, seen here, became the first player to return the opening kick of a Super Bowl for a touchdown in 2007.

SOLDIER FIELD

The Bears play in Chicago, Illinois. Chicago is one of the biggest sports cities in America. Aside from the Bears, it has two famous baseball teams, a basketball team, and a hockey team. The Bears play in a **stadium** called **Soldier** Field. Soldier Field is much more than just a place to watch football. It is a special building that honors American soldiers who have died in wars.

The Bears' team colors are dark blue, orange, and white. All NFL teams have special signs called **logos**. Logos are often worn on the sides of players' helmets. The Bears' logo is a big orange letter C. The C stands for "Chicago."

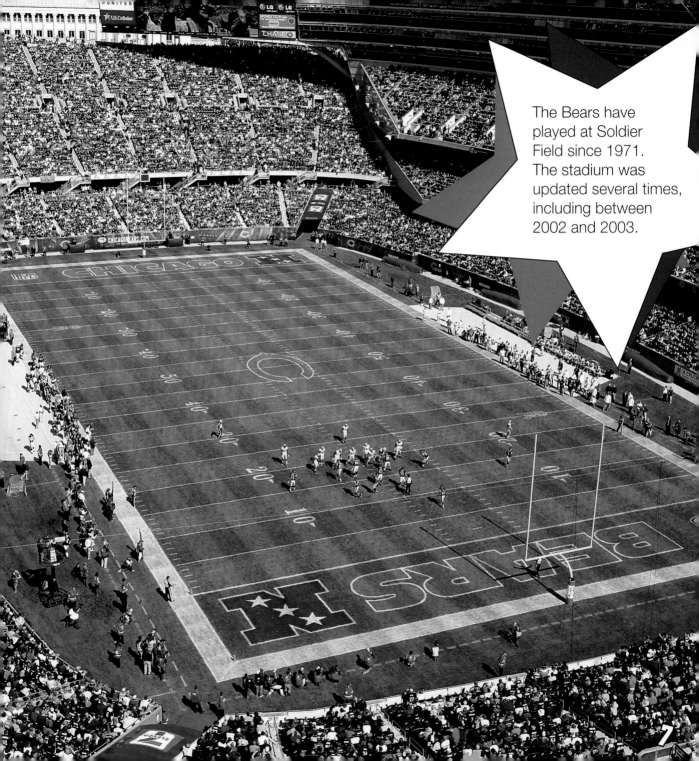

The Bears have played at Soldier Field since 1971. The stadium was updated several times, including between 2002 and 2003.

7

DA BEARS

Bears fans often call the team Da Bears. This nickname comes from the TV show *Saturday Night Live*. Funny actors used to appear on the show dressed as Bears fans. They made fun of the way some people from Chicago talk. When these people say "the Bears," it sounds like "da Bears." Chicago fans loved this part of the show even though it poked fun at them. The Bears are also called the Monsters of the Midway. This is because Chicago is home to the famous Midway Plaisance Park.

The Bears have a very old **rivalry** with the Green Bay Packers. Bears fans love it when their team beats the Packers.

Bears fans love seeing the team's mascot, Staley Da Bear, at games. They also like to sing the team's fight song, "Bear Down, Chicago Bears."

THE DECATUR STALEYS

It might be hard to believe, but there was a time when few people cared about football. Starting a football team was often easier than keeping it in business. In 1919, a company called A. E. Staley formed a football team. A. E. Staley was based in Decatur, Illinois. The team was called the Decatur Staleys.

George Halas soon took over the team and became its coach. In 1921, he moved the team to Chicago. The Staleys played at Cubs Field. This ballpark was later renamed Wrigley Field. The Chicago Cubs baseball team plays there. In 1922, the Staleys were renamed the Bears. The name was picked because baby bears are cubs.

Here, coach George Halas (kneeling) talks to a group of Bears players. Over the years, Halas led the team to win 324 games.

CHAMPIONS

The young team got off to a great start. Excellent players like Red Grange led the team during its early years. The Bears won the NFL **championship** in 1921. In the old days, there was no championship game. The team with the best record was simply the NFL champion.

In 1933, the NFL decided to hold a championship game between the two top teams. This game later became the **Super Bowl**. The Bears won the very first NFL Championship Game by beating the New York Giants.

In 1939, a **quarterback** named Sid Luckman joined the team. He would help the Bears change football forever.

Red Grange, seen here, was known as the Galloping Ghost. This is because he was quick and good at staying away from the other team's players.

13

THE T FORMATION

Luckman and the Bears were so good in the 1940s that they won four championships. Coach Halas used a special plan in the 1940 championship game called the T formation. The T formation surprised the Washington Redskins. The Bears crushed them in that game, 73–0. Other teams then began to use the T formation. The Bears changed the way football was played.

The Bears struggled in the 1950s. In the 1960s, some of the greatest football players of all time joined the team. During these years, players such as Dick Butkus, Gale Sayers, and Mike Ditka led the team to greatness again. The Bears won another championship in 1963.

Dick Butkus, seen here, played linebacker for the Bears between 1965 and 1973. He was both quick and strong.

SWEETNESS

No team can stay on top forever. The Bears struggled again during the 1970s. They got better when they **drafted** Walter Payton in 1975. Payton later became one of the greatest **running backs** ever to step onto a football field. Fans nicknamed him Sweetness because he was such a great player and so well liked.

Sweetness helped the Bears return to greatness in the 1980s. Former player Mike Ditka became the head coach in 1982. He put together a great football team. The Bears changed the game of football again in 1985 with one of the strongest **defenses** in football history. The 1985 team even won the Super Bowl.

Here, Walter Payton carries the ball during the Super Bowl on January 26, 1986. In his time with the Bears, he rushed for a total of 16,726 yards.

SUPER BOWL SHUFFLING

The 1985 Bears team won fans around the nation. They even recorded a **video** for a rap song called "The Super Bowl Shuffle."

Ditka left the team in 1992. The Bears struggled in the 1990s and 2000s. They did not reach the Super Bowl again until 2007.

A new coach named Lovie Smith joined the team in 2004. He helped the Bears return to greatness. The Super Bowl of 2007 was famous because the head coaches of both teams were African Americans. This would be the first time that an African-American head coach would win a Super Bowl. The Bears fell short and lost to a very good Indianapolis Colts team.

Lovie Smith (left) was named the NFL coach of the year in his second season with the Chicago Bears.

700

The Bears bounced back from losing the Super Bowl by winning their seven hundredth game in 2008. The Bears already held the record for most wins. Now they became the first NFL team to win 700 games. They have far more wins than any other team. Many fans believe that no other team will ever win more games than the Bears.

Today, star players such as quarterback Jay Cutler and **defensive end** Julius Peppers have led the Bears back to the top of the NFL. The Chicago Bears continue to make football history. Their fans hope that the Monsters of the Midway will win another 700 games.

Jay Cutler joined the Chicago Bears in 2009. Cutler was a fan of the Bears when he was growing up in nearby Indiana.

CHICAGO BEARS TIMELINE

1920
The Decatur Staleys join what will become the NFL.

1930
The Bears beat the Chicago Cardinals in the NFL's first indoor game.

1939
Sid Luckman joins the Chicago Bears.

1940
The Bears crush the Washington Redskins, 73–0, in the NFL Championship Game.

1964
The Bears pick Gale Sayers and Dick Butkus, two of the greatest football players in history, in the NFL draft.

1968
George Halas retires with more wins than any other coach in NFL history at the time.

1982
Mike Ditka becomes the new head coach of the Bears.

1986
The Bears beat the New England Patriots in the Super Bowl.

2008
The Bears bec the first NFL t win 700 game

GLOSSARY

CHAMPIONSHIP (CHAM-pee-un-ship) Official naming of the best or winner.

COACHES (KOHCH-ez) People who direct teams.

DEFENSES (DEE-fents-ez) When teams try to stop the other team from scoring.

DEFENSIVE END (DEE-fent-siv END) A big football player who tries to stop the other team from scoring.

DRAFTED (DRAFT-ed) Picked for a special purpose.

LOGOS (LOH-gohz) Pictures, words, or letters that stand for a team or company.

PROFESSIONAL (pruh-FESH-nul) Having players who are paid.

QUARTERBACK (KWAHR-ter-bak) A football player who directs his team's plays.

RIVALRY (RY-vul-ree) A struggle between two people or things to see which one is the best.

RUNNING BACKS (RUN-ing BAKS) Football players whose job is to take or catch the ball and run with it.

ER (SOHL-jur) A person who is in an army.

M (STAY-dee-um) A place where sports are played.

OWL (SOO-per BOHL) The championship game of NFL football.

VIH-dee-oh) A short film.

INDEX

WEB SITES

Due to the changing nature of Internet links, PowerKids Press has developed an online list of Web sites related to the subject of this book. This site is updated regularly. Please use this link to access the list:
www.powerkidslinks.com/teams/fbears/